10 MINUTE
SATs TESTS
READING

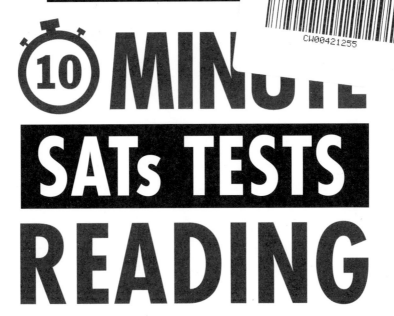

**AGES 10–11
YEAR 6**

KS2

Scholastic Education, an imprint of Scholastic Ltd

Book End, Range Road, Witney, Oxfordshire, OX29 0YD

Registered office: Westfield Road, Southam, Warwickshire CV47 0RA

www.scholastic.co.uk

© 2017, Scholastic Ltd

2 3 4 5 6 6 7 8 9 0 1 2 3 4 5 6

British Library Cataloguing-in-Publication Data

A catalogue record for this book is available from the British Library.

ISBN 9781407176086

Printed and bound in China by Hung Hing Offset Printing

Author
Giles Clare

Editorial
Audrey Stokes, Margaret Eaton, Tracy Kewley, Suzanne Adams

Cover and Series Design
Scholastic Design Team: Nicolle Thomas and Neil Salt

Design
Scholastic Design Team: Alice Duggan

Cover Illustration
Adam Linley @ Beehive Illustration
Visual Generation @ Shutterstock

Illustrations
Adam Linley and Matt Ward @ Beehive Illustration

Acknowledgements
The publishers gratefully acknowledge permission to reproduce the following copyright material: Carcanet Press Ltd for the use of "The Deers' Request" by Elizabeth Jennings from *Elizabeth Jennings The Collected Poems* by Emma Mason. Text © 2012 The Estate of Elizabeth Jennings (2012, Carcanet Press); Ian Souter for the use of "Steaming!" from *Family Poems* by Jennifer Curry. Text © Ian Souter (2002, Scholastic Children's Books).

Photographs
page 15: school dinners, Monkey Business Images/iStockphoto; page 23: Marathon des Sables, J-P Ksiazek/AFP/Getty Images; page 30: dragonflies, M.Fowler, N.Nehring, VitalisG/iStockphoto.

Contents

How to use this book

This book contains ten different Reading tests for Year 6, each containing SATs-style questions. As a whole, the complete set of tests provides broad coverage of the test framework for this age group. Each test comprises a text followed by comprehension questions. The texts cover a wide range of subject matter across the three key areas: fiction, non-fiction and poetry.

Some questions require a selected response, where children choose the correct answer from several options. Other questions require a constructed response, where children write a short or extended answer of their own. Guidance on the different question types and the skills needed to deal with them are covered on pages 48 to 59.

A mark scheme and a progress chart are also included towards the end of this book.

Completing the tests

- It is intended that children will take approximately ten minutes to complete each test.

- After your child has completed a test, mark it and together identify and practise any areas where your child is less confident. Ask them to complete the next test at a later date, when you feel they have had enough time to practise and improve.

The Great Smog of London

In December 1952, a thick layer of yellowy-green smog hung over the city of London for five days. The people of London were used to heavy fogs and smoky air but this was much more serious than previous smog events. It was impossible to see beyond a metre or two, which made driving dangerous or impossible. Public transport was closed down, sports events were postponed and ambulances couldn't reach patients. The smog even affected people indoors: concerts were abandoned and films cancelled because of the reduced visibility in large, enclosed areas. People wore smog masks bought at the chemists and shuffled along trying not to trip over kerbs or other obstacles in the street.

This particular 'pea-souper' was caused by a combination of high pollution, cold winter weather and a lack of wind. The pollutants mostly came from chimney smoke as people burned low-grade coal for heating at home. The cold snap meant more coal was being burned than usual. In addition, there were a number of coal-fired power stations in London, which were belching out thousands of tonnes of carbon dioxide, hydrochloric acid and sulphur dioxide into the atmosphere. Exhaust fumes from steam engines and diesel-powered buses further degraded the air quality. All of this pollution was trapped in the stagnant, cold air under a layer of warmer air, which acted like a lid.

It was only after the smog had blown away that people realised the damage that it had done. An investigation by the medical services revealed that the pollution had made around 100,000 people ill. Shockingly, the smog had also caused the deaths of at least 4000 people. Most of the victims were the elderly or the very young. The main causes of death were lung infections and lack of oxygen. A further 8000 people died in the weeks and months that followed.

The death toll caused a lot of public concern. As a result, the government introduced a number of regulations aimed at reducing air pollution. The Clean Air Act of 1956 created areas in towns and cities where people could only burn smokeless fuels, such as charcoal or gas. The Act also forced power stations to be moved out of town.

Despite these improvements – there hasn't been a major smog in London since 1962 – new research from 2010 shows that around 9000 people a year in the city die early because of air pollution. This time the culprit isn't coal smoke: it is toxic nitrogen dioxide emissions from diesel car engines.

1. Name **one** chemical responsible for air pollution from **each** of the time periods shown.

a. (from the 1950s)

_____

b. (from 2010)

_____

_____

2. Look at the paragraph beginning: *This particular...*
Find and **copy one** word meaning *motionless.*

_____

Marks

1

1

Marks

3. Look at the sentence: *Exhaust fumes from steam engines and diesel-powered buses further degraded the air quality.*
Which **two** words listed below most closely match the meaning of the word *degraded*?

Tick **two**.

improved ☐

contaminated ☐

corrected ☐

polluted ☐

KEEP IT GOING!

1

4. The word *smog* is a combination of two other words. What are those **two** words? Use the first paragraph to help you.

_____

_____

1

5. This kind of smog event was known as a 'pea-souper'. Explain why you think it was called that.

_____

_____

_____

2

6. Look at the sentence: *Most of the victims were the elderly or the very young.* Why do think this was the case?

_____

_____

1

10 MINS

Marks

7. More than one of the following sentences are true, but which **one** best summarises the overall message of the final paragraph?

Tick **one**.

Killer smogs don't happen anymore. ☐

London's air is much cleaner. ☐

London's air is still polluted. ☐

Fewer people are killed by air pollution today. ☐

1

8. Explain how the weather played a part in causing the Great Smog, using evidence from the text to support your answer.

_____

_____

_____

_____

2

Well done! END OF READING TEST 1!

Test 2
Reading

The ride

I remember the moment I made the decision. After the long climb, I was enjoying the cooling breeze on my face, the blur of the hedges and road markings and the thrill of being on that fine line between safety and danger. Until that moment, I had been holding back as usual, sensibly squeezing the brakes each time the bike had threatened to accelerate uncontrollably down the hill.

The slope became steeper and my instincts urged me to tame the racing, rolling beast beneath me. Instead, I made a decision: I let my fingers relax. Given free rein, the bike surged forwards. Gravity was its master now. I leaned lower over the handlebars and felt the air slipping over my sweaty back. My ears were filled with the roar of the wind and the hum of the tyres on the tarmac. My knuckles turned pale on the handlebars, which vibrated and twitched nervously. I could feel my heart thumping in my chest. I peered through narrowed eyes at the road ahead. It was clear. The bike was still gaining speed, but I knew the road would soon start flattening out. I tucked down lower, knifing through the air like a shark through the shallows. A huge smile broke across my face.

A small, dark shape suddenly jumped out from the side of the road ahead of me. It hopped into the middle of the road and stopped. My heart leaped into my throat and before I could think, my fingers wrapped themselves around both brake handles and pulled.

I don't remember what happened after that much, just a few fragmented images and sounds: the hiss and squeal of brakes; the sudden jerk of being launched like a rock from a catapult over the handlebars; the shredded remains of a plastic bag in the top of the hedgerow; the breath being

thumped from my lungs; the cool, sticky mud; and the sudden roar of pain in my ankle.

The doctor told me how lucky I had been. It was just a sprain and my helmet had helped prevent any serious injury. As for my poor aluminium steed, it had been defeated by its fragile, floppy-eared nemesis. I can't wait to get a new one.

1. What kind of animal causes the narrator to crash his bike?

_____

_____

Marks

1

2. What evidence is there that the narrator is hot? Give **two** examples.

a._____

b._____

_____

1

3. **Find** and **copy** a metaphor the narrator uses to describe his bike.

_____

_____

1

4. What does the sentence *My knuckles turned pale on the handlebars* tell the reader about how the narrator was feeling, and why?

_____

_____

1

Marks

5. Look at the sentence: *I remember the moment I made the decision.* What decision did the narrator make?

_____

_____

1

6. Look at the sentence: *I don't remember what happened after that much, just a few fragmented images and sounds.* Explain in your own words what happens during the crash.

_____

_____

_____

2

7. Tick **one** of the boxes below, then answer part **b.** to explain your choice.

a. Do you think the narrator will go so fast on a bike again?

Tick **one**.

Yes ☐

No ☐

b. Explain your choice fully, using evidence from the text.

_____

_____

_____

_____

3

Well done! END OF READING TEST 2!

The Deers' Request

We are the disappearers.
You may never see us, never,
But if you make your way through a forest
Stepping lightly and gently,
Not plucking or touching or hurting,
You may one day see a shadow
And after the shadow a patch
Of speckled fawn, a glint
Of a horn.
　　Those signs mean us.

O chase us never. Don't hurt us.
We who are male carry antlers
Horny, tough, like trees,
But we are terrified creatures,
Are quick to move, are nervous
Of the flutter of birds, of the quietest
Footfall, are frightened of every noise.

If you would learn to be gentle,
To be quiet and happy alone,
Think of our lives in deep forests,
Of those who hunt us and haunt us
And drive us into the ocean.
If you love to play by yourself
Content in that liberty,
Think of us being hunted,
Tell those men to let us be.

By *Elizabeth Jennings*

Marks

1. The poet describes deer as *the disappearers*. Why?

_____

_____

1

2. Name **two** sounds from the second verse that might disturb the deer.

_____

_____

1

3. Look at the line: *Horny, tough, like trees.* Which part of the deer do these words describe?

_____

_____

1

4. **Find** and **copy one** word from the first verse that is both the name of a colour and the name of a young deer.

_____

_____

1

5. Look at the lines: *If you love to play by yourself/Content in that liberty.* Which word in the list below most closely matches the meaning of the word <u>liberty</u>?

Tick **one**.

loneliness ☐

freedom ☐

isolation ☐

power ☐

KEEP IT GOING!

1

Marks

6. What does the advice in the line *Not plucking or touching or hurting* suggest about the forest?

_____

_____

1

7. The poem is called *The Deers' Request*. What is the deer's request?

_____

_____

1

8. More than one of the sentences below is true, but which **one** best summarises the message of the poem?

Tick **one**.

Deer are hard to see in the wild. ☐

People should respect the deer and their habitat. ☐

People should be quiet if they want to see deer. ☐

Deer and people will never get along. ☐

1

9. The deer are described as being driven *into the ocean*. What does this suggest is happening to the place where the deer live?

_____

_____

2

Well done! END OF READING TEST 3!

Should all children have school dinners?

Nowadays, lots of people are worried about what children are eating. There is a lot of evidence that children are eating too many unhealthy, processed foods. Some schools are considering whether to ban packed lunches completely to provide children with healthier food while they are at school. Some people don't like this idea.

On the one hand, research shows that only a tiny percentage of packed lunches meet the same nutritional standards provided by school meals. It was found that most packed lunches contained sweets, sugary drinks and salty snacks such as crisps and only 20 per cent contained the recommended amount of fruit and vegetables. It is a difficult and time-consuming task for parents to provide a healthy-enough packed lunch. Banning packed lunches would save parents the bother every day.

In addition, the quality of school meals has improved significantly in recent years. Schools can also provide better-quality meals at a cheaper price because they are made in bulk. Furthermore, it has also been shown that good-quality, cooked school meals boost children's academic performance, keeping them feeling more healthy and energetic during the day.

On the other hand, many parents believe that school meals cost too much and that they can provide a cheaper packed lunch. Some parents on low

incomes claim they cannot afford to pay for a cooked meal and should not be forced to do it.

Also, other parents argue that it is not the headteacher's job to interfere: it is parents who should be deciding what their children eat. They are not happy with the quality of the cooked school meals provided and believe that the meals still contain too many processed foods. They worry that their children won't like how the school meals taste and won't eat enough to be healthy.

Finally, a few parents insist that they have to provide their children with a packed lunch because their children have allergies or a food intolerance.

I. Name **two** items of food found in packed lunches that are not considered to be good for your health.

Marks

_____

_____

_____

1

2. Using information from the text, tick **one** box in each row to show whether each statement is **fact** or **opinion**.

	Fact	Opinion
School meals cost too much.		
Eating school meals can help children do better at their work.		
Packed lunches often contain foods high in salt or sugar.		
School meals don't taste good.		

1

| | Marks |

3. Look at the paragraph beginning: *On the other hand...*
Find and **copy three** words meaning 'paid a small amount of money'.

_____

_____

1

4. This text is organised as a 'for' and 'against' balanced argument. **Find** and **copy** all the **conjunctions** or **conjunction phrases** that help organise the points. Two have already been done for you.

'For'	'Against'
On the one hand	On the other hand

2

5. Which group of people is said to be against the idea of banning packed lunches?

Tick **one**.

Parents and headteachers ☐

Parents ☐

Teachers and headteachers ☐

Researchers ☐

KEEP IT
GOING!

1

Marks

6. What is missing from 80% of packed lunches?

_____

_____

_____

1

7. What is the benefit of making cooked meals in bulk?

_____

_____

_____

1

8. Some parents say they have to provide a packed lunch. What safety reason is given?

_____

_____

_____

1

9. Which of these sentences best summarises the arguments for banning packed lunches?

Tick **one**.

Packed lunches are bad for you and take a long time to prepare. ☐

School meals are cheaper and make you energetic. ☐

Packed lunches don't contain enough fresh food. ☐

School meals are healthier than packed lunches and help with school work. ☐

1

Well done! END OF READING TEST 4!

Test 5

Reading

The Singing Bone

In a faraway kingdom long ago, the King's lands were terrorised by a giant boar. Every day, the beast destroyed crops and tore villagers apart with its tusks. The desperate King had no choice but to offer his only daughter in marriage to whomever killed the dangerous boar.

Two brothers came forward. The older brother was crafty and vain. His younger sibling was kind and innocent. The brothers entered the forest from opposite sides to improve their chances of finding the demon pig. Very soon, the younger brother encountered a tiny man, who gave him an enchanted spear.

"Because I know your heart is kind, I know this spear will help you in your task," the little man said. Sure enough, the younger brother came across the vicious boar. It charged at him in a rage. The boy held the spear with all his might and the tip split the beast's heart in two. He lifted the giant boar onto his back and made his way towards the castle. At the edge of the forest, he found his older brother drinking in a tavern. The older brother was filled with envy to discover his brother had won the challenge.

"Here, drink some wine in celebration," he said slyly.

A few hours later, they both left the tavern and came to a narrow bridge. "You should cross first for you are the hero!" said the older brother. As his

merry younger brother crossed, the older brother hit him so hard on the back of his head that he fell dead from the bridge. He tumbled onto the muddy river bank below. The older brother returned with the boar to claim his prize, telling the King that his missing sibling had been torn apart by the beast in the forest. The murderous older brother and the princess were soon married.

One day some years later, a shepherd was herding his sheep across a narrow bridge when he saw a snow-white bone sticking out of the river bank. He picked it up and carved it into a mouthpiece for his horn. When the shepherd blew into it, he was amazed as the horn began to sing by itself: a terrible tale of murder.

"I must take this horn to the King," he said.

In the castle, the King listened to the horn's strange song. He suspected at once what had happened. He ordered his soldiers to search the river bank, where they found the rest of the younger brother's bones. As a punishment, the King ordered that the older brother be sewn into a sack and thrown off the bridge into the river.

I. Answer the following questions.

Marks

a. What type of story is this?

_____

b. **Find** and **copy one** phrase as evidence for your answer.

_____

1

KEEP IT
GOING!

Marks

2. Draw lines to **match** each part of the story with the correct line from the text.

Plot twist	The King's lands were terrorised by a giant boar.
Resolution	The brothers entered the forest from opposite sides.
Setting	The horn began to sing by itself: a terrible tale of murder.
Problem	The King ordered that the older brother be sewn into a sack and thrown off the bridge into the river.

1

3. What did the older brother do instead of hunting the boar?

_____

_____

1

4. The older brother is described as *crafty and vain*. **Find** and **copy** a sentence that demonstrates his craftiness.

_____

_____

1

	Marks

5. Look at the paragraph beginning: *A few hours later...* **Find** and **copy one** word meaning <u>brother</u> or <u>sister</u>.

_____

_____

1

6. How did the King know for certain that the older brother had lied about what happened to his younger brother? Explain using evidence from the text.

_____

_____

_____

_____

2

7. Name the **two** magical items in the story.

_____

_____

1

8. Stories like this often have a message about how to behave (a moral). What do you think the moral of this story is? Explain using evidence from the text to support your answer.

_____

_____

_____

_____

2

Well done! END OF READING TEST 5!

Test 6
Reading

Marathon des Sables

It would take you about 20 minutes to walk a mile. Did you know that a marathon is just over 26 miles long? That would mean about nine hours of solid walking just to walk that far! Sounds tough? What about running that distance? What about running two marathons without stopping? That's 52 miles! And what if you had to do it across one of the hottest, most inhospitable environments on earth? The Sahara Desert.

The Marathon des Sables isn't called the toughest foot race in the world for nothing. Each year, extreme athletes sign up to run over 155 miles in six stages over seven days through the endless landscape of the Sahara Desert, where temperatures can reach over 50˚C. As they tackle leg-sapping dunes, rocky hills and scorching salt plains, they are pounded by the relentless sun and the sand fills their shoes and stings their eyes. Most of the athletes alternate between running and walking. Their mouths and throats feel parched and their feet swell and crack in the heat. The runners can't even feel the sweat dripping down their faces because it evaporates so quickly.

> **Race fact:** over 6.5km of elasticated plasters are used to repair the athletes' injured feet.

Not only that, but the racers must also be self-sufficient: they have to carry their own food and equipment for the week on their backs. The only thing

they are provided with is a place in a shared tent at night. Even water is rationed. If they use too much, they are given a time penalty.

> **Race fact:** the athletes consume a total of 120,000 litres of water over the course of the race.

Since the race was established 30 years ago, over 11,000 athletes have been drawn to Morocco to take part. Athletes can enter as individuals or in teams. In such extreme conditions, they forge life-long friendships and raise funds for charities and to help hundreds of local families through education. The event captures the interest of a worldwide audience as it is broadcast in over 200 countries.

> **Race fact:** 'sable' means sand in French.

I. Answer the following questions.

Marks

a. In which desert does the Marathon des Sables take place?

_____

b. In which country does it take place?

_____

_____

2

2. Draw lines to **match** the correct number to each description.

The temperature in Celsius in the desert	52
The number of race stages	30
The number of miles in a double marathon	50
The number of years the race has been going	6

1

3. Look at the first paragraph. **Find** and **copy one** word meaning <u>unfriendly</u>.

Marks

◯ 1

_____

4. Look at the sentence: *Even water is rationed.* Which **one** word in the list below most closely matches the meaning of the word <u>rationed</u>?

Tick **one**.

saved ☐

banned ☐

recycled ☐

restricted ☐

◯ 1

_____

5. There are good and bad things about taking part in the race.

a. What is **one** positive reason for taking part in the race?

_____

b. What is **one** negative problem caused by taking part?

◯ 2

_____

KEEP IT GOING!

Marks

6. What is the only item that the athletes do not have to carry?

Tick **one**.

water ☐

tent ☐

food ☐

clothes ☐

1

7. Name **three** landscape features the athletes encounter during the race.

_____

_____

1

8. Look at the sentence: *Most of the athletes alternate between running and walking.* Why do think that they do this?

_____

_____

_____

1

Well done! END OF READING TEST 6!

Steaming!

I was a slouch on a couch,
watching a favourite TV programme,
when my sister rolled into our lounge
like a gunslinger looking for trouble.
And **with** a smirk and a smile
but **without** a please or a pause
she swaggered over
and simply changed the channels!

Now all day long my sister
had been annoying me.
Filled with devilment,
skilled at annoying,
she thrilled at causing trouble for **me!**
Now here she was – **at it again**
and I'd had enough,
that final snigger had ignited my temper!

Suddenly my anger was a swelling fist,
fire began crackling in my head,
blood began boiling in my brain.
I glared, I stared,
I scowled, I growled.

I wasn't mild – **I was wild!**
I wasn't bad – **I was mad!**
I wasn't dreaming – **I was steaming!**
STEAMING like a train out of control
and just as I was about to derail my temper
my sister smiled knowingly and shouted, **"Mum!"**
And suddenly my anger was braking
my temper was no longer shaking,
my fury was no longer waking
as I realized the risk was not worth taking!
For while my temper is bad
it's not half as wicked
as my **Mum's!**

By *Ian Souter*

Marks

1. Look at the phrase: *my anger was a swelling fist.* What is this an example of? **Circle** the correct option below.

simile   metaphor   alliteration   onomatopoeia

1

2. Find and **copy one** word from the first verse meaning <u>to walk in an arrogant fashion</u>.

1

3. Look at the phrase: *Filled with devilment.* Which word or phrase below most closely matches the meaning of the word <u>devilment</u>?

Tick **one.**

bad behaviour   ☐   sabotage   ☐

playfulness   ☐   mischief-making   ☐

1

Marks

4. What does the phrase *I was about to derail my temper* suggest the narrator was about to do?

_____

_____

_____

1

5. Find and **copy** an example of alliteration from the last verse.

_____

_____

1

6. Look at the line: *my sister smiled knowingly and shouted,* **"Mum!"** Explain what the narrator's sister knew.

_____

_____

_____

_____

_____

2

7. The narrator's sister is *skilled at annoying* him. Explain how you can tell, using evidence from the whole text to support your answer.

_____

_____

_____

_____

3

Well done! END OF READING TEST 7!

Test 8
Reading

The life cycle of a dragonfly

Have you ever seen a dragonfly? Many people think that dragonflies only live for a day, but that's a misconception. It is true that most adult dragonflies in Britain only live for a few weeks, but the life cycle of a dragonfly often lasts more than a year. There are three stages in the dragonfly life cycle:

The egg

Dragonflies mate while flying in the air. The female dragonfly lays her eggs on a plant in the water or drops them into a body of calm water. You may even have seen a dragonfly skimming across a pond and dipping its abdomen into the water.

The nymph

After 2–5 weeks, the eggs hatch and an aquatic larva called a nymph emerges. Dragonfly nymphs live underwater as they grow and develop. The nymphs prefer to live in ponds or marshes where the water is calmer. They are voracious predators: they hunt other invertebrates, tadpoles and even small fish. This is the longest stage of the dragonfly life cycle. For some dragonflies, it can even last four years. During this time, a nymph moults its skin a number of times until it is developed enough to leave the water.

The adult

When the weather is warm enough, the fully grown nymph crawls up a plant stem out of the water and hangs upside down. There it completes its metamorphosis into a dragonfly: its skin splits to allow the adult to emerge. You can sometimes find the shed skin, called the excuvia, left behind on a plant stem. The adult spreads its wings to let them dry out for several hours in the sun until it is strong enough to fly off to hunt for food and search for

a mate. Most adult dragonflies have muted colours for the first few days. After that, they gain their bright adult appearance. Adult life expectancy is short: typically, just a week or two.

Did you know?
In prehistoric times, dragonflies were much bigger. The largest dragonfly today has a wingspan of 19cm; around 250 million years ago, there was a dragonfly with a wingspan of about 75cm!

1. What do many people wrongly believe about dragonflies?

_____

_____

Marks

1

2. Answer the following questions about the stages of a dragonfly's life cycle.

a. Number the stages of a dragonfly's life cycle in the order in which they take place.

adult _____   egg _____   nymph _____

b. Number the stages of a dragonfly's life cycle according to how long each stage lasts (1 for shortest, 3 for longest).

adult _____   egg _____   nymph _____

2

3. Complete the **three** blank boxes in the table.

Time period	
Today	
	75cm

1

Marks

4. Look at the paragraph about the nymph stage. **Find** and **copy** **one** word meaning <u>greedy</u>.

_____

_____

1

5. Why does a dragonfly dip its abdomen into the water when flying across water?

_____

_____

1

6. Look at the sentence: *Most adult dragonflies have muted colours for the first few days.* Which **two** words in the list below most closely match the meaning of the word <u>muted</u>?

Tick **two**.

bold ☐

faint ☐

loud ☐

dull ☐

1

7. What is the *excuvia*? Explain fully with reference to the text.

_____

_____

2

KEEP IT GOING!

8. Why don't nymphs stay underwater to complete their final metamorphosis into an adult?

_____

_____

1

Well done! END OF READING TEST 8!

The chemical spill

Masoud didn't enjoy break times. He tried to join in with tag and football, but he was too slow and clumsy. The other boys would taunt him and call him names. Especially that Usman. Usman the super striker. Usman the clever joker. Usman the big, perfect know-it-all! After a while, Masoud would give up and sneak quietly back inside to see if any of the teachers needed some help.

One day during lunch, Masoud returned to his classroom. He poked his head around the door. His teacher wasn't there. Instead, three boys from his class were standing by one of the desks. They were speaking in low voices. One of them was Usman. Masoud tried to withdraw quietly but he had already been spotted.

"Masoud!" said Usman. "Wait!"

Masoud glanced up at the boys. Usman looked unusually serious.

"Go and find Mrs Collins right now!" said Usman. "There's been a massive chemical spill. Don't come closer. It's really dangerous!" Usman swapped a look with the two other boys, who both nodded vigorously.

Masoud's eyes widened. "What chemical?" he asked.

Usman put his head in his hands. "We're not sure," he replied ominously, "but we think it might be...SODIUM CHLORIDE!"

Masoud gulped. "Sodium chloride!" he repeated.

"There are white crystals all over this table," continued Usman. "Go and tell the teachers, quick!"

"OK, I'm going now!" replied Masoud. He could feel his heart thumping in his chest. He turned and lumbered down the corridor towards the staffroom. Behind him, he heard Usman call out, "Sodium chloride, remember!"

Masoud knocked on the staffroom door, but didn't wait for an answer. Instead, he pushed it open and stepped over the threshold. "Mrs Collins!" he called out loudly.

A dozen teachers looked over at him in surprise. Mr Stark, the deputy head, frowned and said, "Masoud, you can't just burst –"

Masoud interrupted him, "There's been a chemical spill!"

The staffroom fell quiet. "What do you mean? Where?" asked Mr Stark.

"It's all over a table," replied Masoud breathlessly.

"What is?" asked Mrs Collins, his class teacher.

"Sodium chloride! It's sodium chloride!"

For a few seconds, nobody said anything. Masoud could only assume that his news had shocked the teachers into silence. Then he noticed Mr Stark roll his eyes. "Very funny, Masoud," he said. "Sodium chloride, you say?"

Masoud nodded. "Yes, dangerous white crystals!"

Mr Stark shook his head and gave him a pitiful look. "So, what you're telling us is someone's spilt some salt, yes?"

Masoud looked at Mr Stark blankly and then he felt the heat rise up his neck and into his cheeks. Usman!

1. What is the name of the boys' teacher?

_____

_____

Marks

1

2. What trick does Usman play on Masoud?

_____

_____

_____

1

Marks

3. What is the chemical name for salt?

_____

_____

1

4. Look at the paragraph beginning: *Masoud didn't enjoy...* How does Masoud feel about Usman? Use evidence from the text to support your answer.

_____

_____

_____

_____

3

5. *Masoud looked at Mr Stark blankly and then he felt the heat rise up his neck and into his cheeks. Usman!* What emotions does Masoud feel here?

_____

_____

2

6. Look at the sentence: *Masoud tried to withdraw quietly but he had already been spotted.* Why did Masoud not want to be seen?

_____

_____

1

7. Which of the following best describes how Masoud's feelings change from the start to the end of the 'chemical spill'?

Tick **one**.

lonely	→	shocked	→	excited	→	happy	☐
sad	→	annoyed	→	confused	→	relieved	☐
amused	→	scared	→	confused	→	disappointed	☐
nervous	→	worried	→	embarrassed	→	angry	☐

1

Well done! END OF READING TEST 9!

How a chocolate fountain works

Chocolate fountains use an old invention to keep that runny, glossy chocolate flowing.

Firstly, solid chocolate is placed into a metal bowl in the base of the machine. When the machine is plugged in and switched on, a heating element inside the base melts the chocolate. The metal bowl acts as a reservoir for the melted chocolate.

Here's where an ancient Greek inventor comes in.

The machine does not use a pump. Instead it uses a mechanism known as an Archimedes' screw to transfer the liquid chocolate to the summit of the machine. An Archimedes' screw is a mechanism that lifts a liquid from a lower level to a higher level. It is sometimes called an auger and it is similar in looks to a corkscrew.

Next, the melted chocolate is drawn into a cylinder that extends upwards from the bowl. Inside the cylinder is the auger. A small motor turns the auger, which carries the liquid up the cylinder from the bottom until it reaches the top. The cylinder also prevents the liquid from spilling straight back down into the reservoir. When the liquid chocolate reaches the top of the pipe, it spills out evenly over a number of smooth tiers. This creates a cascade of liquid chocolate like a curtain. Edible goodies, such as strawberries, biscuits and marshmallows, can be dipped in the falling chocolate and enjoyed. The rest of the chocolate runs back down into the bowl where the process begins again.

Who was Archimedes?

Archimedes was a Greek mathematician and inventor who was born in Sicily, in Italy, and educated in Egypt. He once made an important discovery about volume when stepping into a bath. It is said he shouted "Eureka!", which means "I've found it!" in Greek. It is thought that he also invented pulleys, catapults and even mirrors that could set an invader's ship on fire.

Marks

1. Name **two** countries where Archimedes lived.

a. _____

b. _____

1

2. Number the processes in the order in which they occur.

The chocolate returns to the reservoir.	
The chocolate is melted in the base unit.	
The chocolate falls over the tiers.	
The auger lifts the chocolate up the cylinder.	

1

3. Look at the paragraph beginning: *Next, the melted chocolate...*
Find and **copy one** adjective meaning <u>something that can be eaten</u>.

_____

1

4. What are the **two** names for the mechanism that lifts the chocolate up the cylinder?

a. _____

b. _____

_____

Marks

1

5. Look at the words: *Firstly* and *Next*... Answer the following questions.

a. What is the job of such words in helping to organise an explanation text?

_____

_____

b. What is the name of these types of words in this context?

_____

_____

2

6. What powers the heating element?

_____

_____

1

7. Where is Archimedes said to have made an important discovery about volume?

_____

1

KEEP IT GOING!

8. Use the information from the text to **label** the parts of the chocolate fountain in the diagram below.

Marks

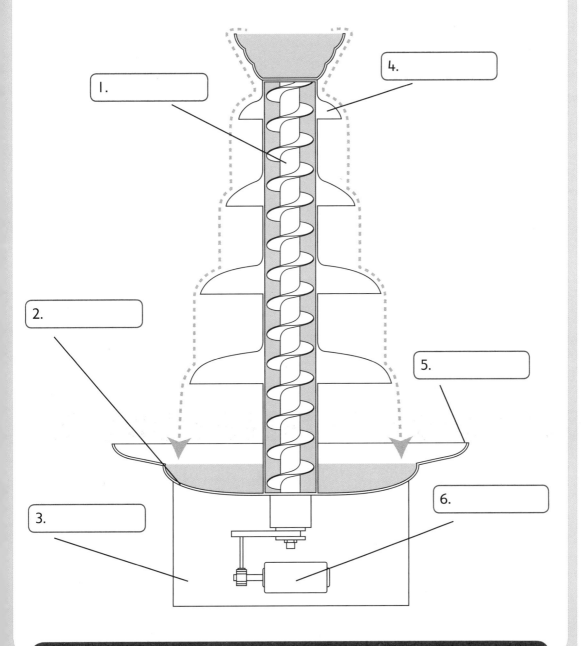

1.

4.

2.

5.

3.

6.

2

Well done! END OF READING TEST 10!

Answers
Reading

Q	Mark scheme for Reading Test 1: The Great Smog of London	Marks
1	**Award 1 mark** (if both correct) for: **a.** carbon dioxide, hydrochloric acid or sulphur dioxide **b.** nitrogen dioxide	1
2	**Award 1 mark** for: stagnant	1
3	**Award 1 mark** (if both correct) for: contaminated; polluted	1
4	**Award 1 mark** (if both correct) for: smoke; fog	1
5	**Award 2 marks** for answers that refer to the smog being similar in **consistency** and **colour** to pea soup. For example: • It is thick/dense/heavy/concentrated. (thickness) • It is green/yellow. (colour) **Award 1 mark** for answers referring to either one of the acceptable points (consistency or colour). Do **not** accept general answers relating to smog being like a soup.	2
6	**Award 1 mark** for answers referring to the comparative vulnerability of both groups to the effects of the smog. For example: They were weaker/They weren't as strong/They were more likely to get infections.	1
7	**Award 1 mark** for: London's air is still polluted.	1
8	**Award 2 marks** for answers referring to the **cold weather** and the **lack of wind** and the **effects** of both. For example: • The cold weather meant people were burning more coal than usual. • There was more chimney smoke than normal because of the cold snap. • There was no wind so the smog was stuck over the city. • The cold smog was trapped under a lid of warmer air and couldn't escape. **Award 1 mark** for answers that refer to either the cold weather OR the lack of wind and their effect. Do **not** accept answers that do not mention the effects of the cold, windless conditions.	2
Total		**10**

Q	Mark scheme for Reading Test 2: The ride	Marks
1	**Award 1 mark** for: rabbit	1
2	**Award 1 mark** (if both correct) for: **a.** cooling breeze on face **b.** sweaty back	1
3	**Award 1 mark** for either: the racing, rolling beast OR my poor aluminium steed	1
4	**Award 1 mark** for recognition that the narrator was gripping the handlebars tightly, which showed fear. For example: Their knuckles were white because they were holding on tight and probably scared.	1
5	**Award 1 mark** for answers referring to the narrator's decision to go faster. For example: They decided to speed up OR They didn't brake as much and went faster. Do **not** accept answers that refer to just going fast.	1

| 6 | **Award 2 marks** for answers that refer to all of the following acceptable points: the narrator braking hard/being thrown over the handlebars/being thrown over a hedge/landing in some mud/hurting their ankle.
For example: The narrator braked hard and was thrown over the handlebars. They flew over the top of a hedgerow and landed with a thump in a muddy field. They injured their ankle.
Award 1 mark for at least three of the acceptable points above. | 2 |
| 7 | **Award 3 marks** for the inclusion of three acceptable points, or two acceptable points with at least one supported by evidence (based on whether the answer to question 7a is yes or no):
a. Yes
b. Acceptable points: the narrator really enjoyed going fast; the narrator can't wait to get a new bike; the narrator wasn't badly injured.
OR
a. No
b. Acceptable points: the narrator is usually more sensible; the narrator had a bad crash; the narrator would be even more scared because of the crash.
Award 2 marks for two acceptable points, or one acceptable point supported with evidence.
Award 1 mark for one acceptable point. | 3 |

Total   10

Q	Mark scheme for Reading Test 3: The Deers' Request	Marks
1	**Award 1 mark** for: because they run away when they are frightened	1
2	**Award 1 mark** (if both correct) for: birds, footsteps	1
3	**Award 1 mark** for: antlers	1
4	**Award 1 mark** for: fawn	1
5	**Award 1 mark** for: freedom	1
6	**Award 1 mark** for answers that suggest the forest is alive and doesn't like being damaged.	1
7	**Award 1 mark** for either: To be left alone/To stop hunting them.	1
8	**Award 1 mark** for: People should respect the deer and their habitat.	1
9	**Award 2 marks** for recognition that the deer's habitat is under threat as a result of human activity. For example: It suggests that people are using more and more space and the size of the deer's habitat is shrinking. **Award 1 mark** for recognition of the threat to the deer's habitat but without reference to human activity. For example: Where the deer live is getting smaller and they are running out of room. Do **not** accept answers that state that the deer live by the ocean.	2

Total   10

Q	Mark scheme for Reading Test 4: Should all children have school dinners?	Marks
1	**Award 1 mark** for two of: sweets, sugary drinks, salty snacks, crisps or processed foods	1

Award 1 mark for:

	Fact	Opinion
School meals cost too much.		✓
Eating school meals can help children do better at their work.	✓	
Packed lunches often contain foods high in salt or sugar.	✓	
School meals don't taste good.		✓

2 — **1**

3 **Award 1 mark** for: on low incomes — **1**

4 **Award 2 marks** if all of the 'for' (In addition, Furthermore) and 'against' (Also, Finally) conjunctions are correctly identified and placed in the table as shown:

'For'	'Against'
On the one hand	On the other hand
In addition	Also
Furthermore	Finally

2

5 **Award 1 mark** for: parents — **1**

6 **Award 1 mark** for: The recommended amount of/enough fruit and vegetables. — **1**

7 **Award 1 mark** for: They can be made more cheaply. — **1**

8 **Award 1 mark** for: Their child might have an allergy or food intolerance. — **1**

9 **Award 1 mark** for: School meals are healthier than packed lunches and help with school work. — **1**

Total — **10**

Q	Mark scheme for Reading Test 5: The Singing Bone	Marks
1	**Award 1 mark for:** **a.** fairy/folk/traditional tale/story (do not accept fiction, legend, fable or myth) **b.** In a faraway kingdom long ago	1
2	**Award 1 mark** for: Plot twist → The horn began to sing by itself: a terrible tale of murder. Resolution → The King ordered that the older brother be sewn into a sack and thrown off the bridge into the river. Setting → The brothers entered the forest from opposite sides. Problem → The King's lands were terrorised by a giant boar.	1
3	**Award 1 mark** for: He went drinking in a tavern/pub (at the edge of the forest).	1
4	**Award 1 mark** for either: "Here, drink some wine in celebration," he said slyly. OR "You should cross first for you are the hero!" said the older brother.	1
5	**Award 1 mark** for: sibling	1
6	**Award 2 marks** for answers that include both the following acceptable points: **a.** The lie that the younger brother was torn apart in the forest. **b.** The reality that the brother's skeleton is found on the river bank. For example: The older brother told the King that his younger brother was 'torn apart by the beast in the forest.' The younger brother's bones were found under the bridge 'on the river bank'. **Award 1 mark** for reference to point (b) but without reference to point (a). Do **not** accept answers that refer only to the mouthpiece/horn.	2

7	**Award 1 mark** (if both correct) for: spear; mouthpiece/horn	1
8	**Award 1 mark** for recognition that you won't get away with bad behaviour or that lies will always be discovered in the end. For example: The moral is that you never get away with the bad things you do because one day they will catch up with you. **Award a further mark** for evidence taken from the story of dishonesty/bad behaviour and punishment. For example: The older brother tricks his brother, murders him and lies to the King. Years later, by chance the shepherd spots the bone and the older brother ends up being thrown into the river in a sack.	2
	Total	10

Q	Mark scheme for Reading Test 6: Marathon des Sables	Marks
1	**Award 2 marks** (if both correct) for: **a.** Sahara **b.** Morocco (do not accept Moroccan) **Award 1 mark** if one of the above is incorrect.	2
2	**Award 1 mark** for: The temperature in Celsius in the desert ➜ 50 The number of race stages ➜ 6 The number of miles in a double marathon ➜ 52 The number of years the race has been going ➜ 30	1
3	**Award 1 mark** for: inhospitable	1
4	**Award 1 mark** for: restricted	1
5	**a. Award 1 mark** for either: making life-long friends OR raising money for charity OR raising money to help local families through education. **b. Award 1 mark** for any of: swollen, cracked/injured feet OR parched mouths and throats OR sand stinging your eyes.	2
6	**Award 1 mark** for: tent	1
7	**Award 1 mark** for: (leg-sapping) dunes, (rocky) hills and (scorching salt) plains	1
8	**Award 1 mark** for: The (hot) conditions/environment would make it too difficult to run all the way.	1
	Total	10

Q	Mark scheme for Reading Test 7: Steaming!	Marks
1	**Award 1 mark** for: metaphor	1
2	**Award 1 mark** for: swaggered	1
3	**Award 1 mark** for: mischief-making	1
4	**Award 1 mark** for: He was about to lose his temper with his sister and hurt her.	1
5	**Award 1 mark** for: blood began boiling in my brain	1
6	**Award 2 marks** if answers include both of the following acceptable points: recognition that the sister knew her brother was about to lose his temper and that she knew her mum would stop him. For example: She knew he was about to attack her and that she could stop it happening by calling her mum. **Award 1 mark** if only one of the acceptable points is mentioned.	2

Q		Marks
7	Award 1 mark for each acceptable point (see below) that refers to the ways used by the narrator's sister to push him to become angry (maximum of 3 marks): ● She interrupts his favourite TV programme on purpose. ● She 'smirks'/'sniggers' at him to wind him up. ● She changes the channel without 'a please or a pause' deliberately to annoy him. ● She smiles at him 'knowingly' when he is about to lose his temper. ● She knows exactly when to shout for her mum to save herself and get him in trouble.	3
	Total	10

Q	Mark scheme for Reading Test 8: The life cycle of a dragonfly	Marks
1	Award 1 mark for: that dragonflies only live for one day	1
2	a. Award 1 mark for: adult 3, egg 1, nymph 2 b. Award 1 mark for: adult 1, egg 2, nymph 3	2
3	Award 1 mark for:	1
4	Award 1 mark for: voracious	1
5	Award 1 mark for: to lay its eggs	1
6	Award 1 mark for: faint, dull	1
7	Award 2 marks for answers giving the correct definition of the excuvia and referring to the change that produces it. For example: The excuvia is the shed skin the dragonfly leaves behind when it completes its final metamorphosis from a nymph to an adult. Award 1 mark for answers that simply refer to shed/dead/old skin.	2
8	Award 1 mark for: They need to dry their wings in the sun.	1
	Total	10

Table within Q3:

Time period	(Largest) Wingspan
Today	**19cm**
250 million years ago/Prehistoric	75cm

Q	Mark scheme for Reading Test 9: The chemical spill	Marks
1	Award 1 mark for: Mrs Collins	1
2	Award 1 mark for answers that refer to making Masoud believe the salt is dangerous and making him tell the teachers. For example: Usman makes Masoud believe there has been a dangerous chemical spill when it's really just salt and tricks him into telling the teachers.	1
3	Award 1 mark for: sodium chloride	1
4	Award 3 marks for answers that recognise that Masoud dislikes Usman and that he is also jealous of him, and that include evidence from the text for both these feelings. For example: Masoud doesn't like Usman because he is one of the boys that call Masoud names. He is also jealous of him because Usman is good at sport (speedy striker) and funny (clever joker). Award 2 marks for answers that include evidence from the text for one of the feelings. For example: Masoud doesn't like Usman. He is also jealous of him because Usman is good at sport (speedy striker) and funny (clever joker). Award 1 mark for answers that recognise that Masoud both dislikes Usman and that he is jealous of him but do not include evidence from the text. For example: Masoud doesn't like Usman. He is jealous of him too. Do **not** accept answers that refer to dislike or jealousy on their own.	3

5	**Award 2 marks** for answers that include recognition that **Masoud is embarrassed** and that **he is angry or annoyed** with Usman for tricking him. For example: Masoud's face is going red because he is embarrassed. He is also probably cross with Usman because there is an exclamation mark. **Award 1 mark** if only one of the acceptable points (embarrassed; angry/annoyed) is mentioned.	2
6	**Award 1 mark** for answers that recognise that Masoud wants to avoid the other boys because he fears they will behave badly towards him. For example: Masoud is worried that he is going to be bullied again by Usman and the other boys.	1
7	**Award 1 mark** for: nervous → worried → embarrassed → angry	1
Total		**10**

Q	Mark scheme for Reading Test 10: How a chocolate fountain works	Marks
1	**Award 1 mark** (if both correct) for: **a.** Sicily/Italy **b.** Egypt	1
2	**Award 1 mark** for: <table><tr><td>The chocolate returns to the reservoir.</td><td>4</td></tr><tr><td>The chocolate is melted in the base unit.</td><td>1</td></tr><tr><td>The chocolate falls over the tiers.</td><td>3</td></tr><tr><td>The auger lifts the chocolate up the cylinder.</td><td>2</td></tr></table>	1
3	**Award 1 mark** for: edible	1
4	**Award 1 mark** (if both correct) for: **a.** Archimedes' screw **b.** auger	1
5	**a. Award 1 mark** for: They help place events/processes in time (chronological) order. **b. Award 1 mark** for: (time) conjunctions	2
6	**Award 1 mark** for: electricity Do **not** accept 'a small motor'.	1
7	**Award 1 mark** for: in the bath	1
8	**Award 2 marks** for: **1.** auger/Archimedes screw **2.** heating element **3.** base unit **4.** tier **5.** metal bowl/reservoir **6.** motor **Award 1 mark** for 4–5 correctly labelled elements. **Award no marks** if fewer than four elements are correctly labelled.	2
Total		**10**

Words in context

Can you...

- give the meanings of words?
- give reasons for your choices?

What you need to know

- There may be more than one meaning for a word. You have to find the word or phrase that is closest to the meaning of the word in a given context.
- The answers are not written in the text but there may be some clues about the word's meaning.
- To answer questions about words in context you may be asked to underline, circle, tick, find and copy information, or write a few words of your own.
- These questions are usually worth one mark.
- There will be between five and ten marks for words-in-context questions in the National Test.

Example

> When I was called into the headteacher's office I anticipated being told off. I had been talking all through the lesson instead of getting on with my work so it was obvious that I had not been sent to his office for a headteacher's award.

1. Circle **one** word that is closest in meaning to *anticipated*.

likely   probable   predictable   (expected)

---

2. Find and **copy** the word that shows the writer did not think there was any other reason to be sent to the headteacher, other than to be told off.

Obvious

Skills check

Retrieval

Can you...

- find information?
- copy accurately?

What you need to know

- 'Retrieval' means to find and write down.
- All the answers will be in the text. You just have to find them.
- The questions are in the order that the answers appear in the text.
- Retrieval answers are usually short and worth one mark.
- You may be asked to underline, circle, tick or find and copy information.
- Retrieval and inference questions together make up most of the marks in the test papers, so make sure you have a go at all these questions.

Example

> It was gone midnight when Tom was awoken by a cat yowling. He felt on his bed, where his own cat Tabitha usually slept. She wasn't there! Anxiously he creeped downstairs to find her. There she was – fast asleep on a cushion under the kitchen table!

1. What time was it when Tom was woken up?

Gone midnight

Just 'midnight' isn't close enough to get the mark.

2. Where did Tabitha usually sleep?

On Tom's bed

3. What was Tabitha sleeping on when Tom found her?

A cushion

You don't need to write 'under the kitchen table' but you would still get the mark if you did. The question only asks what Tabitha was on – the cushion.

Skills check

Summarising main ideas

Can you...

- find the main ideas?
- summarise the main ideas?

What you need to know

- Main ideas are the most important parts of the text: pieces of information or a message (for example, from a poem) that the author wants you to know.
- To 'summarise' a text means to say what it is about in a few words.
- All summarising questions will ask you to find information from more than one paragraph. They could be about the whole text.
- Summary answers are usually short.
- You may be asked to circle, tick, underline or write a few words.
- There will not be more than six summary questions in a full-length test.

Example

> First, a frog lays its eggs in a pond. The tadpoles slowly develop inside the egg and then hatch. When the tadpoles hatch, they are greyish brown, with a head and tail.
> Gradually, over time, the tadpoles will gain back legs, then front legs, their tails will disappear and they will turn greenish.
> The tadpoles are now adult frogs, ready to mate and lay their own eggs in the pond.

1. Summarise in a few words what this text is about.

_____ _The life cycle of a frog_ _____

'Frogs' isn't enough to give the main idea. You need to include a reference to life cycles or reproduction.

Skills check

Inference

Can you...

- make inferences?
- give reasons for your thoughts?

What you need to know

- Inferences are ideas or understanding gained from thinking about what the author doesn't say: you have to work out what the author wants you to think, for example, the message of a text or its moral.
- Inference questions could be about character, place or the writer's attitude to what they are writing about.
- 'Giving reasons' or 'using evidence from the text' means finding something from the text that explains your thoughts and opinions.
- Inference questions might be about the whole text or small parts of it.
- You may be asked to circle, tick, underline or write a few words.
- Inference and retrieval questions together make up most of the marks in the test papers, so make sure you have a go at all these questions.

Example

> Canoeing isn't for everyone. You need to be fit and love water. There are many places to canoe – smooth lakes, rough, fast-flowing rivers and the sea – and all of them involve getting wet! In order to enjoy canoeing safely, the right equipment is needed. A helmet is essential for canoeing down turbulent, rocky rivers, in case you capsize. A life jacket is important, too. You should avoid canoeing on your own. Always make sure before you set out that you have told someone where you are going and when you will be back.

1. Why isn't canoeing for everyone?

      Not everyone is fit and loves water.

2. When canoeing, why should you tell someone where you are going and when you will be back?

      So that people know when and where to start looking for

      you if you get into trouble.

Skills check

Prediction

Can you...

- say what might happen?
- explain your reasons giving evidence from the text?

What you need to know

- 'Predicting' means saying what you think will happen next.
- In order to predict, you need to find out what has already happened.
- Your prediction must be reasonable and likely.
- Prediction questions can often require quite long answers and are often worth more than one mark.
- In a full-length test, there will not be more than three prediction questions.

Example

Northwold, who won the netball tournament last year, are playing at home to Eastleigh this week. Northwold have won all their home games this term whilst Eastleigh have lost all their away games.

1. Based on what you have read, who do you think will win the match this week? Give a reason for your answer using evidence from the text.

Northwold will win easily because they won the netball

tournament last year. They have won all their home

games this term, and they are playing this match at

home; Eastleigh have lost all their away games and this

match is away for them so they are likely to lose again.

Skills check

How information is related

Can you...

- show *where* information is related?
- explain *how* the information is related?

What you need to know

- These questions will ask you to find information from more than one paragraph.
- 'How information is related' means how the text is linked together.
- These questions may ask you to order events, show how themes run through a text or explain how beginnings link to endings.
- In a full-length test, there will not be more than three questions on how information is related.

Example

> The train stopped with a jolt. The passengers hastily caught their flying cups of coffee, books and laptops. This didn't seem right to Harry: they were nowhere near a train station and they had stopped too suddenly.
>
> Harry opened the tiny window above his seat and craned his neck trying to see out. Other people were doing the same and there were mutterings and grumblings as they tried to work out what was going on. And then it all became clear as a bleating noise became louder and Harry saw a large group of sheep being herded away from the tracks, up into the field ahead.

1. Read the first and last sentences. How do they link together?

The first sentence explains that the train has stopped suddenly. The final sentence explains what has caused it to stop.

Skills check

How meaning is enhanced

Can you...

- find *where* meaning is enhanced?
- explain *how* meaning is enhanced?

What you need to know

- 'Enhanced' means made better or made clearer.
- The main way to enhance meaning is to use figurative language such as metaphor, simile, alliteration, assonance, personification and onomatopoeia. Being able to name the parts of figurative language is not enough: you have to be able to explain the effect they have.
- You need to be able to say what the writer is trying to do and how he or she does it.
- You might be asked how a writer builds atmosphere or character, or how the writer persuades you.
- You might be asked about structure or presentation and how these enhance meaning.
- You will usually be asked to find evidence from the text and write about it.
- In a full-length test, there will not be more than three questions on how meaning is enhanced.

Example

When I arrived home, the door was open and my parents were nowhere to be seen. I pushed the door wide open and stood in the hallway. There was a loud crash in my bedroom. I creeped up the stairs like a cat in the shadows, holding my breath.

I creeped up the stairs like a cat in the shadows...

1. What does this phrase tell us about how the writer moved?

    The writer is moving quietly and is trying not to be seen

    or heard.

2. Find and **copy** a phrase from the end of the story that shows how desperate the writer was not to be heard.

    holding my breath

Skills check

Making comparisons

Can you...

- make comparisons to show how things are similar or different in a text?

What you need to know

- 'Comparing' means showing how things are different and how they are similar.
- You may be asked to compare characters, places, opinions or ideas.
- You may have to compare ideas from different paragraphs, or across the whole text.
- You may have to write some sentences of your own. Useful words to use when comparing things are: whereas, however, in contrast, on the other hand, in comparison.
- In a full-length test, there will not be more than three comparison questions.

Example

> Yesterday, I drove past a house I used to live in many years ago. It looked very different from when I used to live there. Although nothing has been added to the building (no extensions or loft conversions), the outside has been painted pale blue and there are new windows and doors. The garden doesn't look as tidy as it used to though! All the trees are overgrown and the new owners have replaced my favourite flowerbed with tarmac.

1. What is the same today as when the writer lived there?

The size and shape of the building – nothing has been added.

2. Give **two** ways in which the garden is not as nice as it used to be.

1. The trees are overgrown.

2. The writer's favourite flowerbed is now tarmac.

Fact and opinion

Can you...

- tell the difference between a fact and an opinion?

What you need to know

- A fact is true and can be proved.
- An opinion is something that someone thinks or believes. It is possible for two people to have different opinions about something.
- Sometimes opinions are written so they look like facts. Watch out for phrases such as 'Everybody knows...' and 'There can be no doubt...'.

Example

> Everybody knows that chocolate cake is the best kind of cake. It's so delicious that most supermarkets sell it. My recipe for chocolate cake contains dark chocolate, cream and sugar, which is why it is the best chocolate cake ever!

I. Put a tick in the correct box to show whether each of the following statements is a fact or an opinion.

	Fact	Opinion
Chocolate cake is the best kind of cake.		✓
Most supermarkets sell chocolate cake.	✓	
The writer's recipe for chocolate cake contains dark chocolate, cream and sugar.	✓	

You need all three ticks for one mark. Watch out for the opinion beginning 'Everybody knows...', which makes the sentence look like a fact. However, chocolate cake cannot be proved to be the best: this is just what the writer thinks.

Skills check

Question types: selected

Selected questions don't ask you to write your own answer. For these questions you need to circle, tick or draw lines.

What you need to know

- **Multiple-choice** questions will ask you to tick a box (possibly in a table) or circle a word or phrase.

- **Ranking or ordering** questions will ask you to write numbers in boxes to order sentences.

- **Matching** questions will ask you to draw lines to make connections.

- **Labelling** questions will ask you to label the features or parts of a text.

- Read the instruction text carefully to ensure that you tick or circle the correct number of options: for example, does the instruction say *Tick **one*** or *Tick **two***? If you tick too many or too few options, you may not get the mark.

- Read all the possible answers, find the relevant information in the text, and check each possibility before deciding on a final answer.

- Carefully cross out any answers you have ticked, circled or labelled in error.

Question types: short answer

These questions require you to write a small amount of text. It might just be a word, phrase or a sentence.

What you need to know

- **Find-and-copy** questions require you to read the text and find a word, phrase or sentences from it that answers the question. You should copy the words exactly. Make sure you read the question carefully so you know which word(s) you are looking for.
- **Short-response** questions require a short answer (a word, phrase or sentence), which will often be in the text.
- These questions are testing your comprehension skills, not your general knowledge. The answer you give should always be based on what you have read in the test paper.
- Practise looking for key words in questions and finding these in the text.

Question types: long answer

There will be some questions that require an open-ended response and are awarded two or more marks. You may have to offer your own opinion and explain your answer. There will not be many of these questions in the test papers.

What you need to know

- Read the question carefully. It is important that you are aware when you need to provide evidence from the text to support your answer.

- Practise reading open-ended questions and planning your answer.

- Try all open-ended questions on the test paper, even if they seem difficult, as they are often worth two or three marks. Even if you don't score full marks, you may be awarded one or two.

Skills check

Test skills

Tips

- Before the National Test, spend time looking over everything that you need to know (for example, the skills check pages of this book). Spend extra time practising the areas that you are less sure of.
- Most of the marks in the reading test will be for identifying information and making inferences, so you may want to spend extra time practising these types of question.
- The amount of time you have in the test includes time for reading the text and answering questions. Find your own strategies for how to manage your time. For example, read and answer questions on one text at a time (there are three texts in each paper of the National test); move onto the next question if you are stuck on one question for a long time.
- Remember, questions come in order of where you can find the answer information in the text: question 1 will relate to the beginning of the text and the answer to question 2 will be found after this, and so on. This will help you find the information you need.
- The questions in each test paper of the National Test get progressively harder. If you are stuck on a question, move on and go back to it if you have time at the end.

Progress chart

Fill in your score in the table below to see how well you've done.

	Score
Test 1	
Test 2	
Test 3	
Test 4	
Test 5	
Test 6	
Test 7	
Test 8	
Test 9	
Test 10	
TOTAL	

Mark	
0–34	Good try! You need more practice in some topics – ask an adult to help you.
35–69	You're doing really well. Ask for extra help for any topics you found tricky.
70–100	You're a 10-Minute SATs Test reading star – good work!

GREAT WORK!

Reward Certificate

Well done!

You have completed all of the 10-Minute SATs Tests

Name: _____   Date: _____

Notes

Reading

QUICK TESTS FOR SATs SUCCESS

BOOST YOUR CHILD'S CONFIDENCE WITH 10-MINUTE SATs TESTS

- Bite-size mini SATs tests which take just 10 minutes to complete
- Covers key National Test topics
- Full answers and progress chart provided to track improvement
- Available for Years 2 and 6

Find out more at www.scholastic.co.uk